WILLIAM AND KATE
A ROYAL ROMANCE

Jane Bingham

Chicago, Illinois

www.heinemannraintree.com

Visit our website to find out more information about Heinemann-Raintree books.

To order:

☎ Phone 888-454-2279

▣ Visit www.heinemannraintree.com to browse our catalog and order online.

©2012 Raintree
an imprint of Capstone Global Library, LLC
Chicago, Illinois

Edited by Louise Galpine and John-Paul Wilkins
Designed by Victoria Allen
Production by Vicki Fitzgerald
Picture research by Tracy Cummins
Originated by Capstone Global Library Limited
Printed and bound in the United States by Corporate Graphics.

15 14 13 12 11
10 9 8 7 6 5 4 3 2 1

Library of Congress Cataloging-in-Publication Data
Cataloging-in-Publication data is available at the Library of Congress.

Acknowledgements
We would like to thank the following for permission to reproduce photographs: Corbis pp. **10** (© Andy Mettler/ Reuters), **32** (© Hulton-Deutsch Collection), **39** (© Sygma); Getty Images pp. **4** (Samir Hussein/WireImage), **5, 6, 7, 8, 9, 38** (Tim Graham), **11** (Toby Melville/AFP), **12** (Stefan Rousseau /WPA Pool), **16** (David Cheskin/ AFP), **18** (Daily Mail/Pool/Anwar Hussein Collection), **21** (Julian Herbert), **23** (John Stillwell/Tim Graham Picture Library), **24** (WireImage), **26** (Simon Maina/AFP), **27** (Chris Ware/Keystone Features), **28** (Photo by Mario Testino/Clarence House Press Office via WireImage), **29** (Danny Martindale/WireImage), **33** (Ben Stansall/AFP), **34** (Anwar Hussein), **40** (Chris Jackson), **36** (Topical Press Agency); Rex pp. **13, 15, 20, 37**; Rex pp. **14** (Ikon Pictures Ltd./Rex), **25** (Davidson/O'Neill), **35** (Nils Jorgensen); Shutterstock pp. **19** (Terry Kettlewell), **31** (R. Nagy).

Cover photograph of the announcement of the engagement of Prince William and Kate Middleton reproduced with permission of Rex (Tim Rooke/Rex).

Contents

Any words appearing in the text in bold, like this, are explained in the glossary.

A royal engagement

On 16 November 2010, a smiling young couple appeared on TV screens around the world. Kate proudly showed off her engagement ring. William described how he had asked Kate to marry him. The exciting news spread rapidly. There was going to be a royal wedding!

A very special couple

William and Kate are no ordinary couple. Prince William is second in line to the throne of Great Britain. His grandmother is Queen Elizabeth II and his father is Prince Charles. When the queen dies, Charles will be king. Then William will rule after Charles. In the future, William and Kate may be crowned King William and Queen Catherine.

William and Kate have known each other for nine years.

All around the world people recognize William and Kate. But what do we really know about them? This book fills you in on the couple. It tells you what they were like when they were children and how they met and fell in love. It also looks forward to their wedding day and their life together after they are married.

Remembering Diana

Kate's engagement ring first belonged to Princess Diana, William's mother. Diana died in 1997, when William was 15. William said he gave Kate the ring so that his mother "didn't miss out" on their happiness together.

Prince Charles and Lady Diana Spencer announced their engagement in February 1981, 30 years ago. Charles was 32 years old and Diana was 19.

Young William

Prince William was born on 21 June 1982. He was named William Arthur Philip Louis, and his family nickname was "Wills" or "Wombat" (the name of a small, furry Australian animal). Baby William had a nanny to look after him, but he spent lots of time with his parents, Princess Diana and Prince Charles.

William and Harry

When William was two years old, his brother Harry was born. The princes lived in London but they often stayed at Highgrove, their country home. Despite their royal upbringing, Princess Diana wanted her sons to enjoy some normal childhood activities. For a treat she sometimes took them to the cinema, and for a meal at a burger bar.

When William was seven years old, he told Harry he wanted to be a policeman when he grew up. Harry replied, "You can't. You've got to be king!"

William was born in St Mary's Hospital in London. Charles and Diana were thrilled.

Time for school

William started nursery school when he was three. Two years later he moved to a **private** primary school. At the age of eight, he went to Ludgrove School in Berkshire, about 80 kilometres (50 miles) west of London. It was a **boarding school**, where the pupils stayed overnight. William was a **boarder** during the week and went home at the weekends.

What was life like in the 1980s?

Margaret Thatcher was prime minister of Britain when Prince William was born. When William and Harry were growing up, the Teenage Mutant Ninja Turtles were very popular on TV, and video games had just been invented. Michael Jackson was one of the biggest music stars of the 1980s.

Harry's (on the right) real name is Henry but he has always been known as Harry.

Troubled times

When William was 10 years old, his parents separated, and four years later they were divorced. Like many children of separated parents, William and Harry had to get used to a new way of life. When they were not at boarding school, they spent some of their time with Princess Diana, and some time with Prince Charles.

Eton College

At the age of 13, William went to Eton College. Eton is close to Windsor Castle, and is one of the world's most famous schools. It was founded in 1440 by King Henry VI. Parents have to pay huge sums of money to send their children there.

Pupils at Eton wear a tail coat, waistcoat, and striped trousers for their school uniform.

A very unusual school

Eton College has many old and unusual traditions. For example, pupils learn to play the Eton Field Game. This is a game rather like football, but it is played with a smaller ball and there is no goalkeeper. The goal is defended by three players, called the "fly", "post", and "bup".

William was a sporting star at Eton. He was the school's fastest junior swimmer and was captain of the swimming team. He did well in his exams, too. By the time he was 18, he had decided to go on to university.

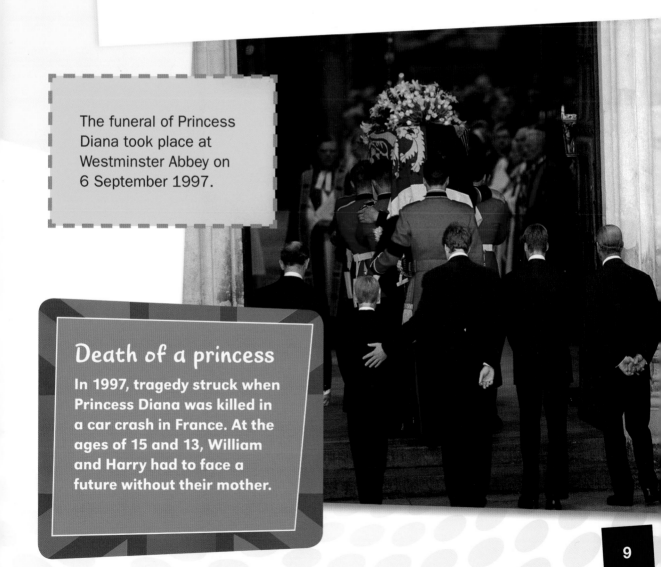

The funeral of Princess Diana took place at Westminster Abbey on 6 September 1997.

Death of a princess

In 1997, tragedy struck when Princess Diana was killed in a car crash in France. At the ages of 15 and 13, William and Harry had to face a future without their mother.

Gap year adventures

After William left school he had a "gap year" before he went to university. He travelled to Belize in Central America, where he took part in a training course with the British Army. He also spent 10 weeks in southern Chile in South America.

In Chile, William helped in a local school. He lived with a group of other young teachers and shared the everyday jobs, such as cooking and cleaning. While he was in Chile, William had a spot as a guest DJ on the local radio station.

"William's star quality is that he's just completely human and normal and one of the gang."

A leader on the project in Chile where William worked in his gap year.

Prince William's gap year was hard work! Here, he is chopping wood at the house he shared in Chile.

The caring prince

William learnt to care for others when he was very young. Princess Diana took William and Harry to visit AIDS clinics and shelters for the homeless. Diana wanted her sons to see that many people had very difficult lives, so they would learn to help others when they grew up. William follows the example of both his parents in his work for charity.

William the sports star

William played a lot of sport in his gap year. Some of his favourite sports are skiing, football, and polo. Polo players ride horses and hit a small ball with a long-handled mallet. They need to be expert horse riders.

In April 2000, Prince William went on a skiing holiday in Switzerland with his father and brother.

Young Kate

Unlike her future husband, Kate Middleton did not grow up in a media spotlight. Kate's parents have always avoided publicity, so not very much is known about her childhood and teenage years.

Meet the Middletons

Kate's parents met when they were working for an airline company. Her mother, Carole, was a flight attendant and her father, Michael, was a flight dispatcher (someone who makes sure that flights leave on time).

Michael and Carole married in 1980 and in 1987 they began to build up a business together. The Middleton's family business supplies all the things that people need for a children's party. Thanks to Michael and Carole's hard work, the business has been very successful.

Kate's parents posed for photographs on the day their daughter's engagement was announced.

Early years

Kate was born on 9 January 1982, and named Catherine Elizabeth. The next year her sister Philippa (known as Pippa) was born, followed four years later by her brother James. Kate spent the first 13 years of her life in Bradfield Southend, a village in Berkshire. Kate went to a local nursery school and joined the village brownies. Bradfield Southend is less than 16 kilometres (10 miles) from Ludgrove, where William was at school between the ages of 8 and 13.

Oak Acre in the village of Bucklebury, is the home of Kate's parents.

A different way of life

Royal children can never enjoy the freedom that Kate had when she was growing up. Kate joined her village brownie pack, but Princess Anne, the daughter of the current queen, had to have a special pack formed for her. The 1st Buckingham Palace brownie pack included Princess Anne and the daughters of people who worked at Buckingham Palace.

St Andrew's School

At the age of seven, Kate became a pupil at St Andrew's School. St Andrew's is a private school for boys and girls, close to Pangbourne on the River Thames. Kate worked hard at her lessons and enjoyed drama, music, and sport.

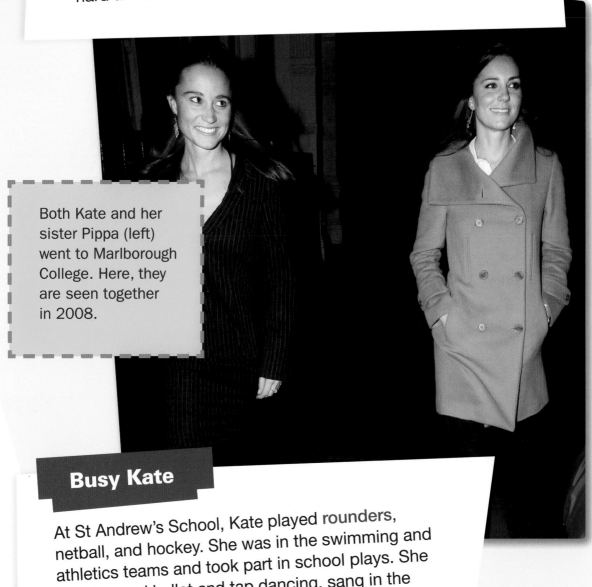

Both Kate and her sister Pippa (left) went to Marlborough College. Here, they are seen together in 2008.

Busy Kate

At St Andrew's School, Kate played rounders, netball, and hockey. She was in the swimming and athletics teams and took part in school plays. She also learned ballet and tap dancing, sang in the choir, and played the recorder.

Changes for Kate

When Kate was 13, her family moved to the nearby village of Bucklebury. In the following year, Kate moved schools to Marlborough College. Marlborough is a mixed boarding school. Just like Eton, it is very expensive.

At Marlborough, Kate was the school hockey captain and was in the top tennis team. For her A levels, she studied Maths, Art, and English, and gained two A grades and a B.

After leaving school, Kate had a gap year. She went to Florence in Italy to study art for three months. In the summer, she worked as a crew member on a yacht.

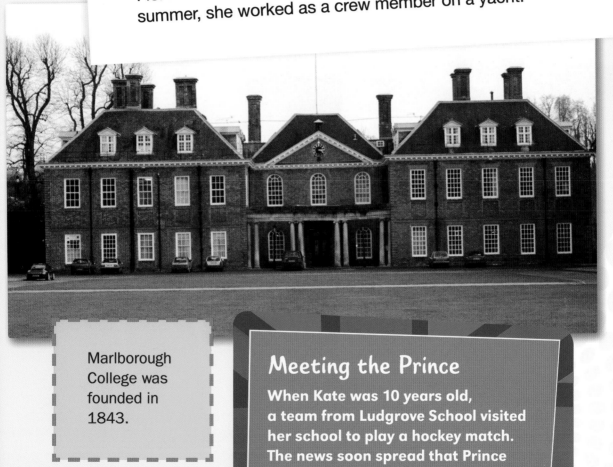

Marlborough College was founded in 1843.

Meeting the Prince

When Kate was 10 years old, a team from Ludgrove School visited her school to play a hockey match. The news soon spread that Prince William was in the team! Kate joined a group of excited girls to watch the match. Later they all crowded round to shake William's hand.

University years

In September 2001, William and Kate arrived at St Andrews University on the east coast of Scotland. They were 19 years old and they were both studying Art History. They attended lectures on the history of painting, sculpture, and other forms of art.

Fun and support

William and Kate soon got to know each other. They belonged to the same group of friends and sometimes played tennis together. When Kate took part in a fashion "catwalk" for charity, William had a front row seat in the audience.

At St Andrews, William was treated just the same as all the other students.

Charles at Cambridge

In 1967, Prince Charles became the first member of the royal family to go to university. He studied History at Trinity College, Cambridge. Many people thought that William would go to Cambridge, too. But William wanted to make his own choices.

Just good friends

During his first year at St Andrews, William had a "wobble". He did not enjoy his course in Art History and he thought he might leave university. Kate encouraged William to stay on and change his course. By the end of the year he had switched to Geography, and he was feeling much happier.

In their second year at university, William and Kate moved into a shared student house. They shared the house with two other friends. At that time Kate had a boyfriend, so she and William were just good friends.

Getting together

William and Kate moved into a cottage with their housemates in September 2003. By Christmas, Kate had split up with her boyfriend. There were rumours that William and Kate were going out together.

In March 2004, William and Kate were spotted together on a skiing holiday. Suddenly their romance became world news. Kate had to get used to photographers taking pictures of her wherever she went.

Student life

Back at St Andrews, William and Kate enjoyed student life. Sometimes they went out to parties, but they also liked to spend quiet evenings at home. Usually Kate cooked for William and their friends, but sometimes William cooked a meal. He admits that he usually ended up burning the food!

Kate attended the same graduation ceremony as William in 2005.

Sporty students

William and Kate both played a wide range of sports at university. In 2004, William became a member of the Scottish universities' water polo team. Water polo players need to call to each other when they pass the ball. The other members of William's team called him "Steve" to make it harder for journalists to notice him.

St Andrew's golf course is very close to the university. It is the world's oldest golf course and is used for international competitions. Prince William enjoys an occasional game of golf but it is not one of his favourite sports. This may be due to a nasty accident he had when he was young (see right).

The Harry Potter prince

When William was eight years old, one of his friends accidently hit him with a golf club. William still has a scar on his forehead, which he calls his "Harry Potter scar".

What next?

In the summer of 2004, William and Kate left university. They both faced the question of what to do next. It was not a hard decision for William. All the men in the royal family spend some time in the **armed forces**. But Kate was not so sure which direction to choose.

Kate's choices

After she left university, Kate had to decide how to use her talents. She had a good degree in Art History. She was a keen photographer and she was very interested in style and fashion. She also had lots of experience of working in her parents' company. In the end, she decided to work for the Middleton family company while she thought about her next move.

After they left university, William and Kate tried to have some privacy, but it was very hard. In October 2005, Kate's lawyers asked the British press to leave her alone.

William in the army

In January 2005, William began his training at Sandhurst Military Academy. The Sandhurst training course is very difficult, but William did well. Fifteen months later he graduated as an officer in the British Army.

Prince William (far right) and his fellow cadets are inspected by the Queen during the Sovereigns Parade at Sandhurst in December 2006.

Tough training

For the first five weeks of their training, new cadets at Sandhurst are banned from leaving camp. They have to get up very early, do lots of physical exercise, and polish their own boots. During their training, cadets learn to use a range of weapons. They are also tested to see if they can survive in the wild.

No war for William

After he left Sandhurst Military Academy, William joined the Blues and Royals regiment. This was the same army unit that Prince Harry had joined. (Harry had gone straight into the army after leaving school.) Most of William's army friends were sent to fight in Afghanistan or Iraq. William wanted to go to a war zone too, but his commanders decided that it was too dangerous to send a future king to war.

Testing times

The year that William joined the army was a difficult period for him and Kate. William was coping with the new challenges of army life, and Kate had just taken on a new job. In 2006, she joined the fashion company Jigsaw as a buyer of accessories such as jewellery and scarves. On top of all this pressure, the couple had to cope with unwanted attention from the press. In the spring of 2007, they decided to separate.

Together again

In the end, William and Kate's separation only lasted for a few months. By mid-summer they were back together again. Kate now sees the time they spent apart as a good thing. She says it made her stronger and more independent.

Royalty at war

In December 2007, Prince Harry was sent to Afghanistan. He served in the war zone for 10 weeks before he was sent home because of threats to his safety. In 1982, William's uncle, Prince Andrew, also served in a war. He was a helicopter pilot in the Falklands War, which was fought on and around the Falkland Islands, close to the coast of South America.

While he was in Afghanistan, Harry took part in expeditions to search for hidden enemies.

Royal Air Force and Royal Navy

In January 2008, William began a new stage in his life. He joined a pilot training course with the Royal Air Force (RAF). This was followed by several months' training with the Royal Navy. These experiences gave him some idea of what life was like in the RAF and the Navy.

"I absolutely love flying … it will be an honour to serve with the Search-and-Rescue Force, helping to provide such a vital emergency service."
Prince William, speaking in an interview on the day he started work as a search-and-rescue pilot.

The pilot prince

By the end of 2008, William had made a decision about his future. He wanted to join the RAF as a search-and-rescue helicopter pilot. William started to train as a pilot in January 2009. His course finished 19 months later in September 2010.

In December 2009, William spent a night on the street to raise awareness for the charity Centrepoint.

Kate and William attended the Boodles Boxing Ball in 2008. It is held in aid of the Starlight Children's Foundation.

Caring for others

As well as serving in the armed forces, William has found time for charity work. Among the many charities he supports are the national AIDS trust and Help for Heroes (an organization that helps soldiers wounded in war). On 22 December 2009, William slept on the street for a night to support Centrepoint, a charity for homeless people in London.

Kate also works for charity. She raises money for the Starlight Children's Foundation, which aims to brighten the lives of children who are seriously ill.

A romantic proposal

In September 2010, William began work as a search-and-rescue pilot. He was based at RAF Valley in Anglesey, North Wales, and he and Kate had a cottage close to the RAF base. By this time Kate was no longer working. The press had nicknamed her "Waity Katy" because she seemed to be waiting patiently for William to **propose** to her!

An African holiday

In October, William and Kate went on holiday to Kenya in Africa. William took Kate to a secret place that can only be reached by helicopter. They stayed in a log cabin beside a lake. The cabin had no electricity and the four-poster bed was made from tree trunks.

William and Kate stayed in these cottages while on holiday in Kenya.

The perfect place

William and Kate stayed by the lake for two days. They went fishing and had a fire to keep them warm. In the evening, the cabin was lit by candles. It was the perfect place for a proposal. On the evening of 20 October 2010, Prince William asked Kate to marry him. When she said yes, he gave her Princess Diana's ring. William had been carrying the ring in his rucksack for three weeks!

Princess Elizabeth in Kenya

Prince William's proposal was not the first historic royal event to take place in Kenya. In February 1952, William's grandmother, then Princess Elizabeth, was staying the night at the Treetops Hotel. The next day she was told the news that her father, King George VI, had died. This meant that she was the new queen.

Elizabeth and Philip were in Kenya when she became queen.

Asking permission

Once William and Kate were back in Britain, William went to visit the Middletons. He wanted to ask Kate's father for his permission to marry his daughter. In the past, men always asked permission from a woman's father before they proposed marriage. So William was keeping up an old tradition, although he had already proposed to Kate. Michael Middleton said yes, of course. He and his wife Carole were thrilled that Kate was going to marry William.

A public announcement

For over three weeks William and Kate kept their engagement secret. Then on 16 November 2010 they made a public announcement. This was followed by an interview that appeared on television and the Internet.

William and Kate had special photographs taken to mark their engagement.

A happy couple

In their interview, William and Kate talked about how they met, and how they had got to know each other's families. Kate said that the Queen and Prince Charles had been very friendly and welcoming to her.

Wonderful news

People everywhere were delighted by the royal engagement. The British Prime Minister, David Cameron, said that when his government heard the news there was "a great cheer and a great banging of tables".

"I just chose when to do it and how to do it and obviously being a real romantic I did it extremely well."
Prince William describing how he proposed to Kate.

William has a great sense of humour and likes to make fun of himself.

William's stepmother, Camilla, Duchess of Cornwall, was thrilled with the news of his engagement. She said it was "wicked"!

Wedding plans

Soon after the announcement of William and Kate's engagement, the date and place of their wedding were decided. It was announced that the royal wedding would be held on 29 April 2011 in Westminster Abbey. This was just the start of five months' planning for an amazing and historic event.

An enormous project

Planning a royal wedding is an enormous project. Long before the great day, invitations have to be sent out. Every detail of the wedding service needs to be rehearsed (practised) until it is perfect. The route that the royal couple will take from the Abbey has to be decided, and safety measures need to be put in place for the crowds. There are flower arrangements to create, music to organize, and menus to be planned for the wedding reception. The bride's dress also has to be designed, made, and fitted.

Wedding planners

Two wedding planners will share the task of making sure that everything runs smoothly. Jamie Lowther-Pinkerton and Helen Asprey are working closely with William and Kate to create the wedding of their dreams.

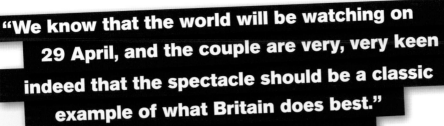

"We know that the world will be watching on 29 April, and the couple are very, very keen indeed that the spectacle should be a classic example of what Britain does best."

Jamie Lowther-Pinkerton, one of the planners for the royal wedding.

Westminster Abbey will be a wonderful setting for the royal wedding.

Westminster Abbey

William and Kate chose Westminster Abbey for their wedding because of its "staggering beauty". It has also provided a stage for royal events for almost 1,000 years. The Abbey stands in the heart of London, close to the Houses of Parliament.

Abbey of kings and queens

Westminster Abbey has a long royal history. The first Westminster Abbey was founded by King Edward the Confessor in the 10th century. Then, in the 1200s, King Henry III replaced the old abbey with the building we see today. A total of 38 coronations have been held in the Abbey. In the 20th century, it began to be used for royal weddings. Princess Elizabeth (who later became queen) and Princess Anne were both married there.

Princess Elizabeth married Philip Mountbatten, Duke of Edinburgh, in Westminster Abbey in 1947.

A "people's ceremony"

William and Kate have said they want their wedding to be a "people's ceremony". Along with their grand and famous wedding guests, they want to invite people from all walks of life. Guests at the Abbey will include children, community workers, and men and women connected with the couple's charity interests.

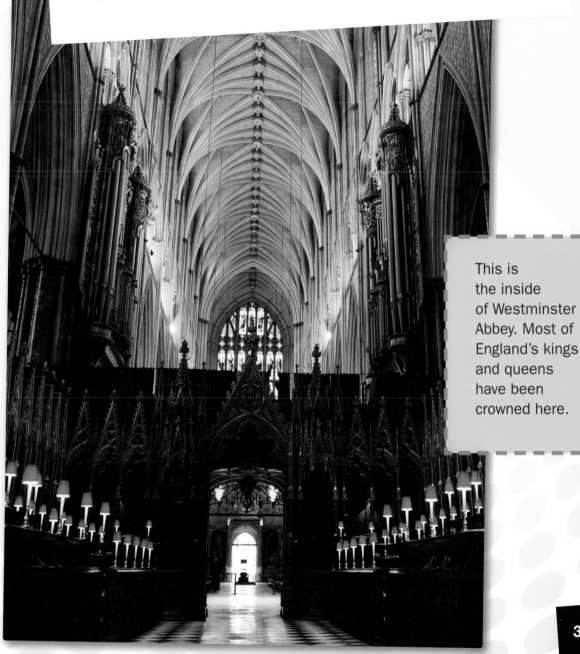

This is the inside of Westminster Abbey. Most of England's kings and queens have been crowned here.

Who will pay?

The royal wedding could cost up to £20 million, but who will pay for it? Prince Charles and the Queen have promised to pay most of the bill and the Middletons will pay for Kate's dress. It is likely that the British people will have to bear the cost of police security for the crowds. They will do this by paying extra money in taxes. Some people are unhappy about this payment. But many others think a national celebration will be good for Britain.

Balcony stars

Queen Victoria set a royal trend when she appeared on the palace balcony during celebrations for the Great Exhibition of 1851. At the end of World War II, hundreds of thousands cheered King George VI and Winstone Churchill on the palace balcony.

Prince Charles and Princess Diana delighted crowds when they kissed on the balcony of Buckingham Palace after their wedding in 1981.

Cutting costs?

Some people have said that Kate and William's wedding should not be too extravagant (expensive). At a time when people are trying to cut costs, the couple may need to think of ways to save money. When Princess Elizabeth got married, in 1947, Britain was recovering from World War II (1939–45). As a way of cutting costs, she and Philip knelt on re-used orange boxes, covered with padded silk.

A holiday for all

Friday 29 April will be a holiday across the UK. Millions of people will gather in London to catch a glimpse of William and Kate. Many others will celebrate with local street parties. There are also plans for firework displays and outdoor concerts. The celebrations will stretch far beyond the UK, as people around the world share in the happy occasion.

The British people love to celebrate a royal occasion. Many will wait all night to catch a glimpse of the wedding procession the following day.

What will she wear?

It is an ancient tradition that the bride's dress must be kept a secret until her wedding day. So we can only guess what Kate's wedding gown will be like. But one thing is certain. People will still remember it in 20 years' time.

Princess Diana's dress was made of a huge amount of material, and her train was almost 8 metres (26 feet) long. That's about the length of two cars!

What style?

Kate has to decide who will design her wedding dress. Her favourite designer is the Brazilian Daniella Helayel, who created the Issa label. However, Kate may prefer to choose a different designer. She also needs to find a style that fits in with the surroundings of Westminster Abbey. Lady Diana's choice of a fairytale, puffball dress worked perfectly in the enormous space of Saint Paul's Cathedral, but it may have seemed out of place in the Abbey.

When Sarah Ferguson married Prince Andrew in 1986, she chose a satin dress that had a train decorated with crystal anchors, in honour of Prince Andrew's career in the Navy.

Keeping the secret

The designer of Kate's wedding dress will need to be very careful about security. When Elizabeth and David Emmanuel designed Lady Diana's dress, they hired two security guards to watch their studio 24 hours a day. At night, the precious dress was kept locked up in an enormous safe.

Wedding jewels

Royal brides wear spectacular jewellery. For her wedding, Princess Elizabeth wore a diamond tiara that had been made for her grandmother, Queen Mary, and two pearl necklaces that had been in the royal family for over 100 years.

Princess Diana, whose name was Lady Diana Spencer before she married, wore the Spencer family tiara and a set of diamond earrings that belonged to her mother. Kate Middleton does not come from a royal or an aristocratic family, so she does not have any grand family jewels. But she will certainly be given some wonderful jewellery for her wedding day.

On her wedding day, Princess Elizabeth wore a beautiful diamond tiara.

Kate the "commoner"

Prince William is taking an unusual step in marrying Kate, because she is a "commoner" (someone without a royal or an aristocratic title). In the past, a prince who was **heir to the throne** was expected to marry either a princess, a queen, or a noble woman. In 1660, the future King James II married a commoner called Anne Hyde. Their wedding was kept very quiet. Anne was smuggled into the palace for their wedding ceremony!

Kate has become a fashion icon and regularly features in fashion magazines. Wherever she goes, she is constantly being photographed by the press.

After the wedding

After their honeymoon, William and Kate will return to their cottage in Wales. William will work as a search-and-rescue pilot. He will also make time for his royal duties, such as visits to hospitals and trips to other countries. Kate will take on some royal duties, too, and they will both do work for charity.

Learning to be royal

Joining the royal family is a huge challenge. Kate says it can feel "nerve wracking", but she hopes to "learn quickly and work hard". She is especially keen to "make a difference" by helping people in need.

In December 2010, William and Kate attended a fundraising concert in aid of the Teenage Cancer Trust.

New names

Once Kate is married, she plans to be known as Catherine, rather than Kate. But what title will she have? As Prince William's wife, her official title will be "Princess William of Wales". She may also be given the rank of duchess, but most people will probably call her "Princess Catherine".

Not the first Queen Catherine

There have been five Queen Catherines in British history. In 1420, Catherine of Valois married King Henry V. In the 1500s, three of Henry VIII's wives were called Catherine: Catherine of Aragon, Catherine Howard, and Catherine Parr. In 1622, King Charles II married Catherine of Braganza. Of all the Queen Catherines, Catherine Howard lasted the shortest time – she was married to Henry VIII for just 19 months, before she was beheaded on his orders.

Future king and queen

In the future, Catherine and William will change their titles. If Charles becomes king, they will be the Prince and Princess of Wales. Then if William becomes king, they will be King William V and Queen Catherine. (Catherine will not have a number after her name because she will be the wife of a king rather than a queen in her own right.) But this is all in the future. For now, William and Kate are looking forward to building a happy life together.

Family trees

Prince William belongs to the royal House of Windsor. This Windsor branch of the British royal family begins with Queen Victoria and her German husband, Prince Albert of Saxe-Coburg and Gotha. The royal family changed their German family name of Saxe-Coburg Gotha to the more British-sounding Windsor in 1917. At that time Britain was fighting World War I and the British public was very anti-German.

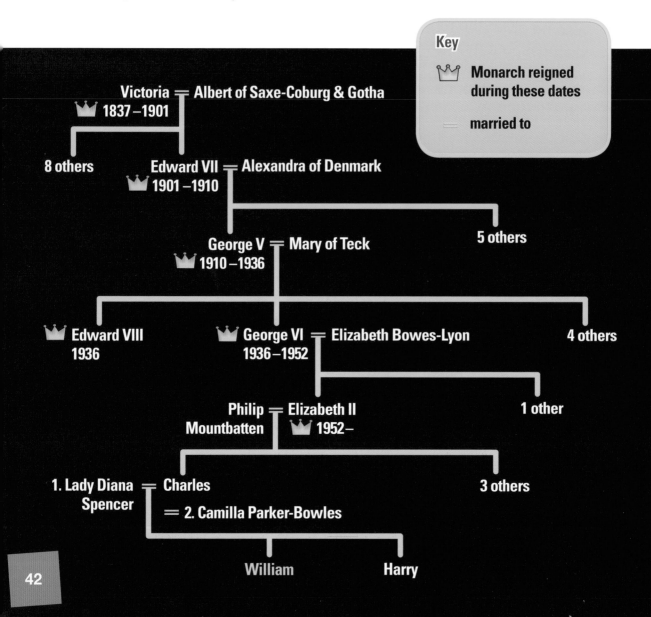

Key

👑 Monarch reigned during these dates

= married to

Victoria = Albert of Saxe-Coburg & Gotha
👑 1837–1901

8 others

Edward VII = Alexandra of Denmark
👑 1901–1910

George V = Mary of Teck
👑 1910–1936

5 others

Edward VIII
👑 1936

George VI = Elizabeth Bowes-Lyon
👑 1936–1952

4 others

Philip = Elizabeth II
Mountbatten 👑 1952–

1 other

1. Lady Diana = Charles
   Spencer
= 2. Camilla Parker-Bowles

3 others

William   Harry

Kate Middleton's ancestors (family in the past) were wool merchants and lawyers on her father's side, and coal miners on her mother's side. Both sides of Kate's family come from the north of England. Her father's family is from Yorkshire and her mother's family is from Durham. One of Kate's great-great-grandfathers, John Middleton, was a successful lawyer, and president of the Leeds Law Society. Another, Francis Lupton, was a very wealthy and successful cloth merchant. This simple family tree begins with them.

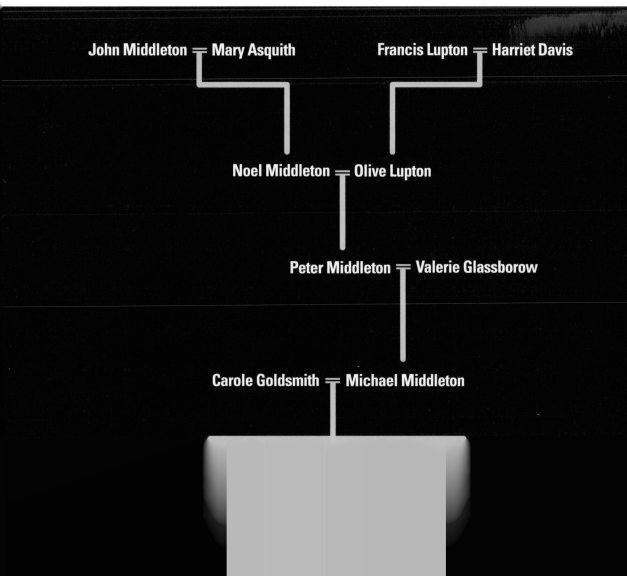

Glossary

accessories something people wear with their clothes, such as jewellery, scarves, and hats

AIDS clinic place where people are treated for AIDS. People with AIDS cannot fight off infections, such as colds and flu, and they become very ill.

aristocratic belonging to a noble family. Aristocrats have titles, such as "lord" and "lady", or "duke" and "duchess".

armed forces military forces that, in Britain, include the Army, Navy, and Royal Air Force (RAF)

boarder boy or girl who stays overnight at a boarding school

boarding school school that provides meals and somewhere to stay during term time

cadet someone who is training for a job in the armed forces

catwalk long raised platform that fashion models walk along so they can be clearly seen

coronation special ceremony to crown a king or a queen

DJ (disc jockey) person who introduces and plays music on the radio or at a club

flight attendant someone who looks after passengers on a plane journey

graduate complete a degree or a training course

heir to the throne someone who could one day become king or queen

interview conversation between a journalist or television presenter and a person of public interest

journalist person who reports on the news or stories of interest to readers or viewers

mallet wooden stick with a head like a hammer. Long-handled mallets are used for hitting the ball in polo matches.

media forms of communication, such as television, radio, newspapers, magazines, and the Internet.

merchant person involved in the trading of goods

officer position in the Army, Air Force, or Navy. Officers are in charge of a group of men and women.

press collective name for newspaper and television journalists

private (school) private schools are not run by the state and parents have to pay to send their children there

propose ask someone to marry you

publicity information about people and their lives presented in the newspapers or on television

reception party for all the guests at a wedding

rounders game played at school involving a bat and ball

security safety measures, to make sure that people are not hurt, or property is not stolen

tax money paid by people to their government so the government can run the country and provide hospitals, schools, and so on

tiara small crown decorated with jewels

tradition certain way of doing things that has happened for hundreds of years

upbringing way that children are looked after and brought up by their parents or by other adults

war zone area in which a war is being fought

water polo game played in a pool with a ball similar to a football

Timeline

9 January 1982	Catherine Elizabeth Middleton is born in Berkshire.
June 1982	Prince William Arthur Philip Louis is born in London.
1983	Philippa Middleton is born.
1984	Prince Harry is born. William goes to a private nursery school in London. Kate goes to a local nursery school.
1987	James Middleton is born.
1989	Kate goes to St Andrews School.
1990	William goes to Ludgrove School as a weekly boarder.
1992	Princess Diana and Prince Charles decide to separate.
1995	William goes to Eton College as a boarder. The Middleton familiy move to Bucklebury in Berkshire.
1996	Princess Diana and Prince Charles divorce. Kate goes to Marlborough college as a boarder.
1997	Princess Diana is killed in a car crash in France.
2000	William and Kate each have a gap year between school and university.
2001	William and Kate meet at St Andrews University in Scotland.
2002	William and Kate move into a student house with two other friends.
September 2003	William, Kate, and their two flatmates move into a cottage close to St Andrews.
December 2003	William and Kate become a couple.
2004	William and Kate are photographed skiing together in Switzerland.
2005	William and Kate graduate from university in the summer. William starts his training at Sandhurst Military Academy. Prince Charles and Camilla Parker-Bowles are married. Kate's lawyers ask the British press to leave her alone.

2006	Kate gets a job as an accessories buyer with the fashion company, Jigsaw. William graduates from Sandhurst as an army officer.
April 2007	William and Kate decide to separate. By June, they are together again.
2008	William trains with the RAF and the Navy. Kate leaves her job at Jigsaw
2009	William starts training as an RAF search-and-rescue pilot. He is based in Anglesey, North Wales.
June 2010	William and Kate move into a cottage close to Angelsey, North Wales.
October 2010	The couple become engaged after William proposes to Kate in Kenya.
November 2010	William and Kate announce their engagement.
April 2011	William and Kate marry in Westminster Abbey.

Find out more

Books

British Kings and Queens (TickTock Books, 2009)

Princess Diana, Joanne Mattern (Dorling Kindersley, 2006)

William and Kate: Celebrating a Royal Engagement,
   Robin Nunn (Pavilion, 2010)

Websites

www.royal.gov.uk/ThecurrentRoyalFamily/PrinceWilliam/PrinceWilliam.aspx
Learn more about Prince William and the rest of the Royal Family
on the official website.

www.britroyals.com/royalfamily.htm
A site on the history of the British royal family.

Index